Phoebe Clappsaddle
and the
Tumbleweed Gang

Phoebe Clappsaddle
and the
Tumbleweed Gang

By Melanie Chrismer
Illustrated by Virginia Marsh Roeder

PELICAN PUBLISHING COMPANY
Gretna 2002

To Evelyn Pansy Massey Karn, my grandmother and my link to Great-Great-Great-Great-Aunt Phoebe Clappsaddle   — M. C.

For my two little Texans, Pratt and Andrew, and Emily, my New Mexican who also loves Texas tall tales —V. M. R.

The word "Pelican" and the depiction of a pelican are trademarks of Pelican Publishing Company, Inc., and are registered in the U.S. Patent and Trademark Office.

Library of Congress Cataloging-in-Publication Data

Chrismer, Melanie.
 Phoebe Clappsaddle and the Tumbleweed Gang / by Melanie Chrismer ; illustrated by Virginia Marsh Roeder.
     p. cm.
Summary: In far west Texas, Phoebe's upbringing as a southwestern belle who can also rope and ride equips her to square off against the meanest, dirtiest, and most ill-mannered cowpokes in the territory.
 ISBN 1-56554-966-X (alk. paper)
[1. Cowgirls—Fiction. 2. Cowboys—Fiction. 3. Behavior—Fiction. 4. Rodeos—Fiction. 5. Chili con carne—Fiction. 6. Contests—Fiction. 7. Texas—Fiction. 8. Humorous stories.] I. Roeder, Virginia Marsh, ill. II. Title.
 PZ7.C4515 Ph 2002
 [Fic]—dc21

                          2002005317

Printed in Korea

Published by Pelican Publishing Company, Inc.
1000 Burmaster Street, Gretna, Louisiana 70053

Phoebe Clappsaddle
and the Tumbleweed Gang

Phoebe Clappsaddle was born in the territory south of Big Spring, west of Marathon, north of Terlingua, and east of El Paso. Phoebe was raised as a Southwestern belle. Her sweet mama taught her Southern manners, and her rancher pa taught her Western skills.

Young Phoebe could ride and rope anything, and did.

Growing up, she rounded up rattlesnakes wherever they hid. And they did. No matter what, she used perfect manners and always kept her pinkies up. Miss Phoebe also created flame-thrower chili—hot and dee-licious! She served it with Southwestern-belle skill. Phoebe was like a blooming cactus, feminine but always able to make her "point."

Every year a rodeo came to the territory, and three brothers came, too. Folks didn't know where the brothers came from . . . originally. They blew into town one day, and like tumbleweeds caught on a fence, they hung around. Folks called Clifford, Elmo, and Eustace the Tumbleweed Gang.

These brothers were the meanest, dirtiest cowpokes in the territory. They acted like wild critters, and all that mattered to them was winning. When it came to the rodeo or chili cookoff, they were serious. Phoebe was serious, too. At this rodeo, the honor of the territory was at stake.

The first rodeo event was the chili cookoff. Eustace Tumbleweed wasn't a rider or roper. His brothers would say, "Eustace, you're no use to us at all except in the chuck wagon." The chili cookoff was his event, strange ingredients and all.

The judges tasted each entry, and they survived Eustace's. The Tumbleweeds snickered when Phoebe's chili was tasted. They had tampered with her recipe.

Even so, flame-thrower chili turned out to be the best
in the territory.

The hogtying contest was next and Elmo Tumbleweed was sure he'd win. Just as it was every year, he gulped air as the calf was released and roped the animal in time to burp. He loved burping in public, making the womenfolk faint. He set the time to beat and celebrated by burping even louder. Phoebe was next.

When the calf was released, she raced her horse, Julep, toward it. Her pink lariat landed gently around the calf's neck.

Hopping off Julep, she skipped to the calf, neatly tied three legs together, and curtsied. She beat Elmo without losing a curl. That sissified sight made the Tumbleweed Gang shudder.

"Wouldn't that sugar your grits?" grumbled Clifford.

Now, Clifford Tumbleweed was a broncobuster. He'd pick his teeth with a cactus needle while hanging onto a wild bronco. No horse could throw him off, and this time, he broke his old record. But not leaving anything to chance, he switched Phoebe's bronco to a dangerous horse called Dyn-o-mite.

The crowd gasped when the bronco snorted in the shoot. Showing no fear, Phoebe dusted off Dyn-o-mite's back and whispered in the horse's ear.

"What in tarnation? Quit that girlie nonsense! Yep!" whined the Tumbleweed Gang.

The crowd held its breath.

Instead of Dyn-o-mite exploding from the shoot, he walked out like a plow horse.

Phoebe was named grand champion and blew kisses to the crowd.

"That rips it," said Clifford.
"No more mister nice fellers," added Elmo.
"Yep!" concluded Eustace. To lose the rodeo to a girl was too much!

The brothers decided to get rid of Phoebe Clappsaddle. Eustace stole Julep and Clifford scribbled a note. Elmo wrapped it around a rock and delivered it through Phoebe's front window.

The note read:

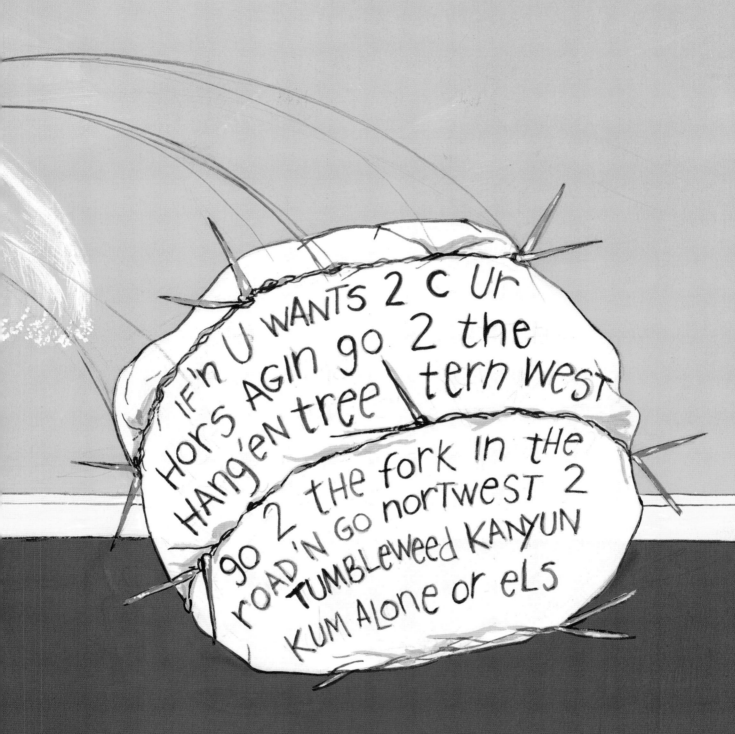

Phoebe hoped Julep was all right, but she was worried about the Tumbleweeds. This was not the proper form for an invitation.

Hitching the surrey to her other horse, Mint, Phoebe headed west. No one was going to get away with horse-napping Julep.

She was a lady, but if the Tumbleweed Gang could not be handled with politeness, her pioneer spirit would take over.

When Phoebe came to Tumbleweed Canyon, she spotted Julep in a corral with three scruffy horses, near an outhouse and a cabin.

A sign out front said BeWare ov Dawg, and lying under it was a critter that was at least part dog. When Phoebe came closer, the dog lifted an eyebrow and three rifles poked out at her.

"That's fur enough, Clappsaddle," warned Clifford, picking his teeth.

Elmo burped, "We've got you now, girlie."

"Yep," said Eustace with a cackle.

"Gentlemen, I have come for my steed," said Phoebe.

"What's a steed? All we got is her horse," Elmo said.

"Yep," said Eustace.

"Quiet, you two! She means her horse," complained Clifford. He took the cactus needle out of his mouth and put it in his back pocket. "We'll return your nag, when you leave the territory."

"I do not take kindly to bullying," answered Phoebe. "Release my horse or I will use force."

At this, Clifford frowned, Elmo spat at a bug, and Eustace snorted. The Tumbleweed Gang hollered together, "Clappsaddle, you asked for it!"

Phoebe said, "Let the games begin."

Whistling for Julep, she sprang from the surrey with a basket in her hand. Julep pranced over and nuzzled the gate latch open.

Phoebe stepped into the corral and opened her basket. She fanned the smell of hot biscuits, prickly pear marmalade, and chili toward the cabin.

Completely overpowered and drooling, Eustace stumbled to the surrey. A clove-hitch knot secured him.

Next, Phoebe sprang to Julep's saddle and went after Elmo. He was hogtied in record time and burp-silenced with a perfumed bandanna.

Clifford yelled, "Sick 'em Dawg."

Too late. Just as Dawg turned, Phoebe tamed him with a long-overdue ear scratching. Frustrated, Clifford ran to his horse, but he didn't remember the cactus needle in his back pocket.

When he hit the horse's bare back, they both got the "point." The horse bounced Clifford around the corral, bucking him off and through the outhouse roof.

As the afternoon shadows lengthened, the Tumbleweed Gang sat in the dirt trying to figure out what had gone wrong. Meanwhile, Phoebe made sure Dawg and the horses were fed and watered, secured the corral, and prepared the cabin for mealtime.

"Wash up for supper, Tumbleweeds," Phoebe said.

A bit later, Clifford, Elmo, and Eustace clanged their spurs through the door. The Tumbleweed Gang almost looked human.

After supper, the brothers escorted Phoebe back to town. On the way, she found Clifford, Elmo, and Eustace as hungry for knowledge as they had been for her food.

They sheepishly asked Phoebe to teach them her Southwestern skills and recipes.

"I'll do that," said Phoebe, "if y'all learn some manners, first. And if you three behave yourselves, I'll toss in reading, writing, and arithmetic lessons."

"Then I can write a better ransom note!" exclaimed Clifford.

"I can count how many womenfolk faint when I burp!" agreed Elmo.

"Yep, and I can read a cookbook!" added Eustace.

After that, the Tumbleweed Gang settled down to doing one mean thing a month. And for a time, the desert bloomed in the territory south of Big Spring, west of Marathon, north of Terlingua, and east of El Paso.